FIRST PUBLISHED IN 1991 BY THE STATIONERY OFFICE
FOR THE OFFICE OF PUBLIC WORKS

THIS REVISED EDITION 2002 BY DÚCHAS THE HERITAGE SERVICE,
DEPARTMENT OF THE ENVIRONMENT AND LOCAL GOVERNMENT

Photographs and text compiled by
John Scarry, Dúchas The Heritage Service.
Design by Creative Inputs
Printed by Colorprint Ltd

ISBN 0755712757

Dúchas The Heritage Service

CONTENTS

FOREWORD TO THE PHOTOGRAPHS

Office of Public Works internal memo, 1877

All of the photographs reproduced in this book are from the Photographic Archive of Dúchas The Heritage Service, Department of the Environment and Local Government. Most of them were printed from quarter plate glass and film negatives, some were contact-printed from whole plate glass negatives, and some of the earliest, dating from around the 1860s, were re-photographed from faded prints where no negative exists. The later photographs from the 1930s are from the more familiar 6 x 9 centimetre format roll film.

The post-1850s period saw a rapid expansion in the use of photography in the Irish countryside. Although a number of photographic studios had been established over a decade earlier, their main business was recording the family portrait. These studios used a silver plate process, the daguerrotype, named after its French inventor, Louis Jacques Mandé Daguerre (1789-1851). This utilised a sensitized coating on silver or silver on copper plate. An alternative process was the calotype paper negative system first demonstrated by William Fox Talbot in England in 1839. The calotype had an advantage over the daguerrotype in that multiple copies could be made from the negative, but copyright restrictions limited its more widespread use. By 1860, superior quality wet-plate negatives were being used, followed in the late 1870s by the much less cumbersome dry glass plates. These later innovations meant that photography in Ireland would no longer be the sole preserve of a few wealthy people.

As this collection pre-dates the establishment of a photographic unit in the Office of Public Works (OPW), who were originally responsible for the protection of National Monuments, the prints and negatives were acquired from different sources. Some would have been taken by members of the inspecting staff of the OPW of the time, while members of the Royal Society of Antiquaries donated others. The Office of Public Works also commissioned a number of photographic firms, including T. P. Geoghegan of Sackville Street, Dublin, Ward and

Dear Sir I forward you today the
Parcel Post the Photos of Ancient
Monuments ordered in yours of 2/3/95
2 Sets, except in the Case of Views Nos
1352 & 1353 of which only one copy each
is sent those negatives being mislaid &
not obtainable at present.
I am not sure whether the Deerpark
Memorial Sligo forms part of the
Carrowmore Series visited in the Board.
But I send the View in Chance they are.
Please return if not required.
Yours truly,
R J Welch

Letter from Robert John Welch

of the Welch collection, are housed in the Ulster Museum, Belfast. The photograph of Roscrea Castle on page 69 is from a Laurence print. The Lawrence collection of negatives is housed in the National Photographic Archive of the National Library of Ireland.

Part of the work of caring for any building or monument involves recording how it looked at any given time. In the 17th and 18th centuries many artists and engravers recorded ancient sites, often using some artistic licence to 'improve' the appearance of their subject. The arrival of photography in the mid-19th century provided a revolutionary way of recording subject detail accurately and almost instantly, something we now take for granted. Today, with modern techniques, photography plays an important part in recording historic sites for conservation, restoration and archaeology.

Every year many thousands of people visit the monuments of Ireland. Many of the photographs in this book show these just as they looked in the late 19th and early 20th century, often in a poor state of preservation. Nevertheless these photographs are the earliest objective visual record of these monuments and the people that visited them.

Company of Cork and R. J. Welch of Belfast. Robert John Welch (1859-1936) was contracted by the Office of Public Works to photograph monuments in County Kilkenny in July 1914 and on the 14th of that month he also visited Clonmacnoise, Co. Offaly (see pages 12 and 13). Two other photographs by him of Carrowmore and Knocknarea, Co. Sligo, which were acquired by the Office of Public Works at that time, are included in this book (pages 53 and 64). The original negatives of these, along with the rest

v

CARING FOR MONUMENTS
THE STATE'S ROLE IN THE EARLY YEARS

Letter to Robert Cochrane

CARING FOR MONUMENTS

Provision for the care of monuments in Ireland began in 1869 with the passing of the Irish Church Act. The Kilkenny Archaeological Society, a body that has evolved into the Royal Society of Antiquaries of Ireland, had carried out work before this with very limited resources. For instance, £180 was spent at Jerpoint Abbey in 1857, and the east window of the Franciscan Friary, Kilkenny, was opened up under the direction of Thomas Drew, who gave his services free. Much other good work was done by this Society which, in this respect, was the forerunner of what developed into the National Monuments Branch of the Office of Public Works.

The primary objective of the Irish Church Act of 1869 was to dis-establish the Church of Ireland. Churches still in use, with their graveyards, were vested in the Representative Body of the Church of Ireland. Most other graveyards were handed over to Burial Boards, whose powers were subsequently taken over by local authorities. Some of the disused structures in graveyards were considered too interesting to be left unprotected, so the category of 'National Monument' was devised to provide for them.

The Commissioners of Public Works were given the job of looking after these monuments for which a lump sum of £50,000 was set aside out of funds in the hands of the Church Temporalities Commissioners. The transfer to the Commissioners of Public Works of these ecclesiastical buildings was subject to a ban on their use as places of worship. This ban on their use for religious purposes has remained to this day, subject to some exceptions where there has been a tradition of such ceremonies, such as the annual pattern day at Clonmacnoise.

The Irish Church Act became effective as regards its ecclesiastical provisions at the beginning of 1871. However, the beginning of the Commissioners of Public Works' concern with National Monuments dates from 27 October 1874, when the '*ruins of the Ancient Cathedral Church on the Rock of Cashel with the land adjacent thereto*' were vested by the Church Temporalities Commissioners in '*the Secretary of the Commissioners of Public Works in Ireland*'.

DR. ROBERT COCHRANE
INSPECTOR OF NATIONAL
MONUMENTS 1899-1916

DR. HAROLD LEASK
INSPECTOR OF NATIONAL
MONUMENTS 1923-1948

By the end of 1874 thirteen more monuments had been vested, including Monasterboice, the Ahenny Crosses and Glendalough. The first Inspector of National Monuments, or Superintendent as he was then called, was Mr (later Sir) Thomas Newenham Deane, one of a well-known family of architects, who took charge in March 1875. Works at Cashel, Ardmore, Glendalough and Ardfert then started without further delay. Most of the Irish Church Act vestings were architectural monuments, but there were also a number of dry-stone buildings, such as the Aran forts and the beehive huts and stone cashel at Inishmurray. The Ancient Monuments Protection Act for Britain and Ireland was passed in 1882, adding a further batch of monuments to the care of the Commissioners. This specified, in a schedule, a number of monuments which were not ecclesiastical, the owners of which could, if they so wished, appoint the Commissioners as owners or guardians. The distinction between ownership and guardianship continues to this day; about one third of the monuments in the care of Dúchas The Heritage Service are not owned by the State but have been placed by their owners in State guardianship.

The scheduling of a monument under this Act allowed the Commissioners to proceed against anybody **except the owner** in the event of its being damaged or destroyed, completely ignoring the fact that the owner was the very person most likely to do damage in the course of developing his property! A classic instance occurred in the early 1900s when the owner of the Hill of Tara was persuaded to allow a band of British Israelites to dig up a large part of the Rath of Synods in the belief that they would find the Ark of the Covenant buried there. There was nothing the Commissioners could do to stop them.

In 1892, the Ancient Monuments Protection (Ireland) Act extended the provisions of the 1882 Act so that additional ecclesiastical monuments could be vested or taken into guardianship, since it was realised that not every worthwhile monument of this kind had been vested by the Irish Church Act. Another development was under the Land Acts of 1903 and 1923. If any land vested in a purchaser under the Land Purchase Acts contained any monuments which, in the opinion of the Land Commission, were important, the Land Commission could make an order vesting such monuments in the Commissioners of Public Works. Castles were, generally speaking, rather under-represented, as compared with prehistoric or ecclesiastical monuments until the 1930s, when Harold Leask conducted a campaign to rectify this imbalance.

After the death of Sir Thomas Deane in 1899 his post was filled by Dr Robert Cochrane, described in the Annual Report as 'one of our Principal Surveyors', a term which was then used to describe the Commissioners' Architects. In 1911-12 the Royal Society of Antiquaries of Ireland, of which Dr Cochrane was at that time President, made strong representations to the Chief Secretary, Augustine Birrell, about the inadequacy of the existing legislation on the conservation of monuments and, in particular, the disappointing results of the provisions of the 1903 Land Act.

It had been hoped that a Royal Commission similar to those being appointed for England, Wales and Scotland to prepare inventories of monuments worthy of preservation would also be appointed for Ireland. These hopes achieved nothing, the excuse being that 'having regard to the contemplated changes in the Government of Ireland' the question of a Royal Commission for Ireland should be left for the consideration of an Irish government at some future time.

In 1916 Dr Cochrane died in his 71st year. He had done admirable work in the recording of monuments. His county guides to Cork, Wexford and Westmeath, which each appeared as appendices to the Annual Report, may be taken as examples, as may his series of articles on the ecclesiastical antiquities of Howth which he published in the Journal of the Royal Society of Antiquaries of Ireland. Cochrane's successor, Andrew Robinson, held office in the troubled period from 1916 to 1923, during which the Annual Reports were, not unnaturally, brief and meagre. After the passing of the Government of Ireland Act 1920, twenty-two monuments were transferred from the care of the Commissioners to the Works division of the Ministry of Finance in Northern Ireland, overseen by Dr D. A. Chart. (In 1976 the responsibility for Monuments work was moved

from the Department of Finance when the Historic Monuments and Buildings Branch of the Department of the Environment (N.I.) was created.) In 1926 the Ancient Monuments (N.I.) Act was passed. This Act provided for the reporting of all archaeological finds, a provision adopted by Dáil Éireann in the 1930 National Monuments Act. In October 1923 the Commissioners appointed Dr Harold Leask as the Inspector of Monuments. He was, like his predecessors, only a part-time Inspector and spent much of his time designing new buildings, such as national schools. With the passing of the National Monuments Act of 1930 he became the full-time Inspector of National Monuments.

Between 1882 and 1930 there were two categories of monuments – National Monuments under the 1869 Irish Church Act and Ancient Monuments under the 1882 Ancient Monuments Protection Act. The funds for Ancient Monuments were voted by Parliament, while National Monuments continued to be maintained out of the lump sum provided by the Church Temporalities Commissioners. The National Monuments Act of 1930 abolished the rather meaningless distinction between Ancient Monuments and National Monuments and all were henceforth to be called National Monuments and to be maintained out of the annual vote.

A monument was defined as 'any artificial or partly artificial building, structure, or erection whether above or below the surface of the ground and any cave, stone, or other natural product whether forming part of, or attached to, or not attached to the ground, which has been artificially carved, sculptured or worked upon or which (where it does not form part of the ground) appears to have been purposely put or arranged in position and any prehistoric or ancient tomb, grave or burial deposit, but does not include any building which is for the time being habitually used for ecclesiastical purposes'. This was a long and cumbersome definition, but it survived the test of time fairly well. (The 1987 Amendment Act, however, extended the definition to include a group of buildings etc., a ritual, industrial or habitation site, and any place containing the remains or traces of buildings etc.)

Having defined a 'monument' the 1930 Act went on to define a 'National Monument' as '*a monument or the remains of a monument, the preservation of which is a matter of national importance by reason of the historical, architectural, traditional, artistic or archaeological interest attaching thereto*'. An important new provision in the 1930 Act provided for the Minister for Finance to make a Preservation Order, where, in his opinion, a National Monument was in danger of being or actually was being destroyed, injured or removed or was falling into decay through neglect. The 1954 Act delegated this power to the Commissioners.

A Preservation Order did not permit the Commissioners to do works to the monument in question, but if they felt that works were necessary they could become Guardians of the monument. This allowed them to spend public money on conservation works without interfering with the ownership of the property.

The prohibition on unlicensed archaeological excavations was another important advance achieved by the 1930 Act. In Northern Ireland the Ancient Monuments Act of 1937, adopted from the 1930 Act, the provision for licensing archaeological excavations, something that is still absent from legislation in Britain.

Further amendments have been made to the National Monuments Acts in the decades since the 1930's to cover such areas as Maritime Archaeology and to place legal restrictions on the use of metal detectors.

In 1997, responsibility for National Monuments was transferred from the Office of Public Works and became the responsibility of Dúchas The Heritage Service, in the Department of Arts, Heritage, Gaeltacht and the Islands. In 2002, Dúchas The Heritage Service became part of the Department of the Environment and Local Government.

THE RAVAGES OF TIME

NEWGRANGE PASSAGE TOMB, CO. MEATH, IN 1908
Even before modern research revealed its archaeological and
astronomical significance, Newgrange was Ireland's best known
prehistoric monument.

THE RAVAGES OF TIME

ROSS CASTLE. KILLARNEY, CO. KERRY, C. 1870
Built by one of the O'Donoghue Ross chieftains, this 15th century tower
was held by Lord Muskerry and the Royalists in the Cromwellian wars.
A barrack block was built against the south wall in the 18th century.

GLENDALOUGH ROUND TOWER, CO. WICKLOW, IN 1875
An ecclesiastic settlement was founded in Glendalough by St Kevin, a 6th century saint. One of the most striking remains is the round tower, over 30 metres high. In 1876 the conical cap was rebuilt, using the original stones.

CARRICK-ON-SUIR CASTLE, CO. TIPPERARY, C. 1890
Thomas, Earl of Ormond, built a Tudor mansion, one of a handful in
Ireland, in 1568 onto an earlier 15th century castle which contained four
towers and a curtain wall around a square enclosure. The Tudor mansion
contains elaborate plaster friezes depicting Thomas Butler with
Queen Elizabeth I and King Edward.

THE RAVAGES OF TIME

QUIN FRIARY, CO. CLARE
Overhanging branches give an eerie appearance to the extensive
remains of this Franciscan friary, supposedly the first Franciscan house
in Ireland following the Observantine rule. The remains also cleverly
incorporate part of the fabric of a Norman castle

'ST COLUMB'S HOUSE', KELLS, CO. MEATH IN 1910
This oratory with its steep stone roof is associated with the famous ecclesiastic settlement of Kells founded by St Colmcille in the 6th century. The entrance is modern, the original structure was entered by a door in the west wall.

ST PATRICK'S ROCK, CASHEL, CO. TIPPERARY
The round tower dates from about 1100. The cathedral is an aisleless
building of cruciform plan, with a later tower added. The row of lancet
windows seen here are typical of an Irish 13th century building.

ST. PATRICKS ROCK, CASHEL, CO. TIPPERARY
The north doorway into Cormac's Chapel has a tympanum, rare in Ireland, depicting a centaur wearing a Norman helmet, shooting with a bow and arrow. This doorway was the main entrance to the chapel until the 13th century cathedral was built alongside the chapel.

CHURCH ISLAND, LOUGH GILL, CO. SLIGO
The remnants of a medieval church mark the site of a 6th century
foundation of St Loman's. A fire, which destroyed the church in 1416,
burned the total O'Cuirnin Library.

JERPOINT ABBEY, CO. KILKENNY
One of the finest Cistercian monasteries, it was founded in 1150 and
became a daughter house of Baltinglass Abbey in 1180. The abbey was
partly reconstructed and the tower added in the 15th century.

TWO LITTLE BOYS AT LISLAUGHTIN FRIARY, CO. KERRY
Founded in 1478 by John O'Connor Kerry for the Franciscans, the fine triple sedilia is visible in the photograph on the right of the choir.

CLONMACNOISE, CO. OFFALY, 14 JULY 1914
One of Ireland's foremost early ecclesiastic settlements which was
founded by St Ciaran in the 6th century. The remains are still extensive
and form a picturesque group on the banks of the River Shannon. This
photograph shows, from left to right, the cathedral, Temple Finghin with
attached tower, the roof of the Church of Ireland church, and
O'Rourke's Tower.

THE CROSS OF THE SCRIPTURES, CLONMACNOISE, CO. OFFALY
This photograph, taken on 14 July 1914, shows one of the finest high crosses in Ireland. Much later, conservation works were carried out to the graveyard.

AN UNKNOWN LADY AT MUCKROSS FRIARY, CO. KERRY
The best-preserved of the Franciscan friaries, it was founded in 1448
and completed about 1475. It contains a preserved cloister with an old
yew tree in the centre. The friars were finally driven out when the
monastery was burnt by the Cromwellians in 1652.

THE RAVAGES OF TIME

CONG ABBEY, CO. MAYO
This photograph shows a group of people in front of the cloister range of
the Augustinian Abbey said to have been built by Turlough O'Connor,
king of Connacht in the 12th century.

THE INTERIOR OF DUNBRODY ABBEY, CO. WEXFORD, 19 JULY 1895
The tower of this Cistercian abbey was added in the 15th century.

ST DOULAGH'S CHURCH, CO. DUBLIN
Note the square tower of this unusual medieval church which is dedicated to St Doulagh, a 7th century hermit.

INCH ABBEY, CO. DOWN
A kilometre north west of Downpatrick. This photograph which is
credited to J. Phillips of Belfast, shows the 12th century Cistercian abbey
before conservation works were carried out.

**AN UNUSUAL VIEW FROM THE EAST OF DUNLUCE CASTLE,
CO. ANTRIM, C. 1870**
Situated beside the coast road between Portrush and Bushmills, the
earliest parts of the castle probably date from the 14th century although it
is not documented until the 16th century, when it was in the hands of the
MacQuillans and later the MacDonnells.

'LEAC AN SCAIL', KILMOGUE, CO. KILKENNY.
Portal Dolmen with a steeply sloping capstone. Note the graffiti on
the sidestone.

TO REPAIR AND RESTORE

KILMACDUAGH, CO. GALWAY

Many of the round towers of Ireland were struck by lightning. The Annals refer to damage to O'Rourke's great bell tower at Clonmacnoise in 1134. The ecclesiastic settlement of Kilmacduagh was founded early in the 7th century by St Colman, son of Duogh, a member of one of the local royal families. It has one of the finest collections of churches in Ireland. This photograph was taken before repairs were carried out under the supervision of Sir Thomas Deane. From his report to the office, made in the year 1879, the following extract is taken:

'The condition of this structure was such as to render it a matter of much consideration whether repair was possible.

Its leaning position, and the dangerous rent running nearly from top to bottom, made it no easy matter to secure its safety. A large portion of the overhanging and crumbling masonry was carefully removed, and re-instated with the original stones; the dilapidated capping has been restored, and it is now perfectly safe.'

TO REPAIR AND RESTORE

ARDMORE, CO. WATERFORD
Showing the restoration of the round tower in 1875-76. The original monastery was founded here by St Declan, a 5th century bishop. The round tower was probably built in the 12th century, and is one of the finest in Ireland.

TO REPAIR AND RESTORE

**DONAGHMORE, CO. MEATH,
CHURCH AND ROUND TOWER**
The early efforts of the Office of
Public Works at looking after
monuments in State Care resulted in
the rescue of many of these ancient
structures from ongoing ruin and
collapse. St Patrick is said to have
founded the first monastery here at
Donaghmore.

The round tower lacks its characteristic
top windows, these may have been
omitted when the conical cap was
replaced early in the 19th century. In
this picture the repairs are being
carried out to the later medieval church
on the site.

TAGHMON, CO. WESTMEATH, CHURCH, 1925
Carefully examining the doorway of this 15th century fortified church dedicated to St Patrick, note the medieval head over the keystone.

TO REPAIR AND RESTORE

DOWTH PASSAGE TOMB, CO. MEATH
Work in progress at the entrance to the tomb in 1932. There are two
chambers, one cruciform, with many decorated stones, in the great
mound. The site suffered severely from the attentions of treasure seekers
and road-makers and unlike its neighbours in the Boyne Valley it has not
yet been archaeologically excavated or restored.

GRANGEFERTAGH ROUND TOWER, CO. KILKENNY
This is one of the photographs taken for the Office of Public Works in July 1914 by Robert Welch. The 30-metre-high tower had been damaged by fire in 1156.

**WORKMEN ON THE EXCAVATION OF LABBACALLEE WEDGE TOMB,
CO. CORK IN 1934**
This was the first excavation conducted under a new Government
scheme for the relief of unemployment and was directed by
H.G. Leask and Liam Price. The rate of pay for the men was one
guinea (€1.33) per week.

SCATTERY ISLAND, CO. CLARE
Precarious repairs were in progress when this picture was taken on 16 March 1916. The ecclesiastic settlement, which overlooks the town of Kilrush, was founded in the 6th century. It suffered greatly from Viking raids and may even have been occupied by them until its recapture by Brian Boru. The most conspicuous part of the monastery is the round tower, which is unusual in that the door is at ground level. To the east of the tower is the cathedral, a church with antae or projecting side walls and a lintelled doorway.

ST MOLUA'S CHURCH, CO. CLARE
The small partially stone roofed oratory of St Molua on Friar's Island in
the Shannon was threatened in 1929 with total submersion as a result of
the Shannon Hydro-Electric scheme. A site was found in Killaloe, high
above the river, and the church was carefully re-erected, every stone
having been numbered.

VISITS AND EXCURSIONS

INISHMORE, CO. GALWAY, ABOUT 1897
An Aran Islander stands beside the well-preserved stone oratory of
Temple Benan. It has a distinctive Early Christian flat-headed doorway,
and the side walls are built with exceptionally large stones. The site is
associated with St Benan, a disciple of St Patrick.

NEWGRANGE, CO. MEATH, ABOUT 1910
Suitably attired for the day's outing, the lady and child stand behind the
famous decorated stone marking the entrance to the tomb.

BREASTAGH OGHAM STONE, CO. MAYO

J.D. La Touche and Robert Cochrane visiting this impressive pillar stone in 1898. The damaged inscription probably commemorates the grandson of a 5th century local king, Amalngaid. The stone was re-erected in 1853.

DUNBRODY ABBEY, CO. WEXFORD
Dunbrody is one of the longest Cistercian abbeys in Ireland. Some of its domestic buildings also remain. It was founded in 1175 by Hervey de Montemarisco, an uncle of Strongbow.

VISITS AND EXCURSIONS

KILMALKEDAR CHURCH, CO. KERRY
This photograph shows a number of people arriving for a funeral service
at the Romanesque church.

**ROMANESQUE DOORWAY,
KILMALKEDAR CHURCH, CO. KERRY**
The tympanum of this 12th century
doorway has a head on one side and
an imaginary beast on the other.

CROSS, TORY ISLAND, CO. DONEGAL, 1907
Another excursion, this time to remote Tory Island. The group relax in front of an unusual undecorated T-shaped cross which is associated with a round tower and other scanty monastic remains. There are also 'Cursing stones', said to have been effectively used in 1884 when a gunboat was sunk during its effort to land troops to collect rates from the islanders.

AUGUSTINIAN PRIORY, KELLS, CO. KILKENNY
Two ladies dressed in the costume of the day about 1897 at
the 12th century priory. Most of the existing buildings date from
the 15th century.

VISITS AND EXCURSIONS

CLOGHAN NEAR SLEA HEAD, CO. KERRY
This is not an early structure but was built in the ancient style about
1900 by local farmers, probably to house animals.

WOMAN AT THE DEERSTONE, GLENDALOUGH, CO. WICKLOW
One of the many legends of Glendalough concerns the deer who, at
St Kevin's request, shed her milk into this hollow granite basin to feed
the motherless twins of one of Kevin's workers.

VISITS AND EXCURSIONS

EARLY ECCLESIASTIC SETTLEMENT, INISHGLORA, CO. MAYO
Two local fishermen pose at one of the pilgrims' 'stations' associated
with the 6th century monastery founded by St Brendan the Navigator.

MONASTERBOICE, CO. LOUTH, EARLY ECCLESIASTIC SETTLEMENT
A funeral service at the site of the monastery founded by St Buite in the 6th century. The cross of Muiredach here is probably the finest of all the Irish high crosses. The round tower, containing a monastic library and other treasures, was burned in 1097. This photograph dates from the 1880s.

DR GEORGE STOKES AND THE REV. D. MURPHY AT GALLARUS ORATORY, DINGLE, CO. KERRY IN 1899
This dry-stone structure is the most perfectly preserved of the boat-shaped oratories.

GLENCULLEN, CO. DUBLIN, PILLAR STONE
Mr Peter O'Neil standing beside the quartz stone. Traditionally known as
Clochnagon: 'the Stone of the Hounds'.

SKELLIG MICHAEL CO. KERRY
Showing Little Skellig on the right-hand side of the picture. This island
ecclesiastic site was founded in the 6th or 7th century. Lying thirteen
kilometres from the mainland its monastic enclosure contains two
dry-stone oratories and six dry-stone cells. It was abandoned in the
12th century but continued as a place of pilgrimage throughout the
medieval period.

49

GRIANAN OF AILEACH, STONE FORT, CO. DONEGAL
Three visitors at the walls of the monument. Legend says that this tall
circular stone structure was built by the ancient gods, but though its date
is unknown, it was probably built sometime in the early centuries of the
Christian era.

VISITS AND EXCURSIONS

CASTLEMARY, NEAR CLOYNE, CO. CORK. CIRCA 1900
Leaning on the megalithic tomb.

**MELLIFONT ABBEY, CO. LOUTH,
11 JUNE 1897**
St Malachy of Armagh brought a
handful of monks with him from
France to found the first Irish
Cistercian monastery here in 1142. Of
the structures only the lavabo and
chapter house survive. We see here
the elaborate south window of the
chapter house.

CARROWMORE, CO. SLIGO, MEGALITHIC CEMETERY, 27 AUGUST 1894
A youthful face beside ancient stones. One of the surviving tombs at
Carrowmore, the largest Stone Age cemetery in Ireland.

GLANFAHAN, SLEA HEAD, DINGLE, CO. KERRY
The photograph of the two boys was taken in one of the cathairs at the
entrance to a souterrain. Souterrains were used both as a means of
escape and for cool storage.

TWO LOCAL GIRLS AT DUNBEG PROMONTORY FORT, CO. KERRY
The fort has four outer defensive banks of stone and earth. Inside is a strong stone wall which had two phases of construction, the inner section being older. A souterrain runs from the lintelled entrance in the stone wall towards the front of the defences.

CLONONY, CO. OFFALY, SHOWING THE 16th CENTURY CASTLE
The arrival of motor transport in the early 20th century afforded easier
access for some people to historic sites.

VISITS AND EXCURSIONS

**THE WEST DOOR OF THE WEST CHURCH, KILLEVY, CO. ARMAGH,
24 SEPTEMBER 1908**
Killevy was one of Ireland's most important early nunneries, founded in
the 5th century. The massive lintelled doorway being 'guarded' in this
photograph is later and dates from the 10th or 11th century.

MAYNOOTH, CO. KILDARE
The ivy shrouded gatehouse of Maynooth Castle, stronghold of the
Fitzgeralds, the Earls of Kildare, until 1707. The coat of arms of the Earl
of Kildare, coupled with those of Richard Boyle, Earl of Cork who
acquired Maynooth, appear above the archway.

ARDMORE CATHEDRAL, CO. WATERFORD
The west wall, shown here, has unusual Romanesque sculptures within
a series of arcades. The church dates mainly from the 12th century.

GRAIGUENAMANAGH ABBEY, CO. KILKENNY
This picture, taken in 1927, shows R. A. S. Macalister, Professor of Celtic Archaeology at UCD from 1909-1943, leading a group of antiquarians on a visit to the two high crosses in the graveyard. The cross in this picture came from Ballyogan, and has representations of King David, the Sacrifice of Isaac, Adam and Eve, and the Crucifixion on the east face and spirals on the west.

MATTHEWSTOWN PASSAGE TOMB, CO. WATERFORD, 1911
Some of the original kerbstones remain though the covering mound is
completely gone.

GURRANES, CO. CORK, STONE ALIGMENT, 1913
This stone alignment in West Cork is known locally as the 'Finger Stones'.

KERNANSTOWN, CO. CARLOW, DOLMEN
Better known as Browneshill Dolmen, it is the largest dolmen in Ireland.
The capstone is reputed to weight over 100 tons.

KNOCKNAREA CO. SLIGO 1894
This massive stone cairn, associated with the legendary Queen Maeve,
the fiery queen of Connacht, probably conceals a Stone Age
passage tomb.

CLONKEEN, CO. LIMERICK, 1925
Peeping out through the Romanesque doorway.

DRUMCANNON CHURCH CO. WATERFORD
Situated about three kilometres from Tramore this photograph shows the medieval church and the Protestent church, which was built onto the east end in 1735. These ruins have deteriorated since the photograph was taken, with the fine bellcote on the west gable now gone.

IN THE TOWNS AND VILLAGES

ROSCREA, CO. TIPPERARY, SHOWING THE 13th CENTURY CASTLE
The rectangular gate tower had a portcullis and drawbridge. The
upper storey was altered in the 16th or 17th century and the curtain
wall which encloses a courtyard (in which stands Damer House), has
two D shaped towers.

ARDFERT CATHEDRAL, CO. KERRY
This cathedral dates from the 13th century but incorporates part of the
west end of a 12th century Romanesque cathedral, comprising a
doorway and blind arcading. The south transept is a later addition.

HOLYCROSS ABBEY, CO. TIPPERARY
This Cistercian abbey has some of the finest stone building of the
15th century in Ireland. Remains include ribbed vaulting and fine traceried
windows. The north transept has one of the few medieval wall paintings
which survive.

CARLOW CASTLE

This must have been one of the finest Norman castles, but only two of the original four towers of this large keep remain. The castle was captured by Cromwell in 1650 but was later returned to its previous owner, the Duke of Thomond.

BOYLE ABBEY, CO. ROSCOMMON, 18 DECEMBER 1894
A cultivated garden beside the remains of Boyle Abbey is a reminder of
the early monks' efforts to be self-supporting farmers dedicated to a life
of prayer. Here, in 1161, beside the River Boyle, the Cistercians founded
one of the most important abbeys in Connacht.

KILKENNY CASTLE, TAKEN FROM THE PARADE
The present exterior of the castle dates mainly to the 19th century.
The castle still retains much of its early quadrangular form with
rounded towers at the corners. It was first built by William Marshall in
the early 13th century, and became one of the castles of the powerful
Butlers of Ormonde.

IN THE TOWNS AND VILLAGES

**DROGHEDA, CO. LOUTH,
ST MARY D'URSO**
During the Middle Ages, Drogheda
was one of the most important English
towns in Ireland. Here, in Old Abbey
Lane, are the remains of the church of
the Augustinian Crucifers Priory and
hospital of St Mary D'Urso, founded
in 1206.

ASKEATON FRIARY, CO. LIMERICK, 23 JULY 1895
One of the photographs taken by the firm of T.F. Geoghegan shows
the late 14th century Franciscan friary. It was plundered in 1579 but
revived again in 1627 and continued to be used by the friars until as
late as 1714.

**CLONDALKIN, CO. DUBLIN,
ROUND TOWER ABOUT 1900**
A ecclesiastic settlement was founded
here around the 7th century by
St Cronan. It was plundered by the
Vikings in 832. The fine round tower
is the most striking of the remains.

ATHLONE, CO. WESTMEATH, CASTLE
Athlone is an important communications centre at the principal
Leinster/Connacht crossing of the Shannon. The original town grew up
in the shadow of this strong medieval castle which commands the
crossing from the west bank.

SLIGO TOWN, FRIARY

The sun shines brightly on the overgrown remains of the town's sole surviving medieval monument. The friary was founded in the middle of the 13th century for the Dominicans by Maurice FitzGerald, who was also founder of the town.

LUSK, CO. DUBLIN, CHURCH AND ROUND TOWER
The impressive remains of the medieval church of Lusk look down on a
neat row of thatched houses. Of the Early Ecclesiastic Settlement,
founded on the site by St Macculin about A.D. 500 only the round
tower, incorporated into the medieval structure, remains.

IN THE TOWNS AND VILLAGES

KING JOHN'S CASTLE, CARLINGFORD, CO. LOUTH C.1902
The railway bridge leads to the shattered but impressive remains of
Carlingford Castle. In the Middle Ages a settlement grew up here under
the shadow of the castle, first built in the 12th century by Hugh de Lacy.

ST AUDOEN'S CHURCH, HIGH STREET, DUBLIN CITY, 1913
The church was dedicated to the Norman Saint, Ouen of Rouen, and was once the leading parish church in the city. The square tower contains the three oldest bells in Ireland, dated to 1423. Archaeological excavation has shown that since medieval times the ground level has risen by over four metres.

DUBLIN. ST AUDOEN'S CHURCH. 1913

THE WALLS OF DERRY AND THE WALKER MONUMENT C.1860
These famous walls have withstood several sieges, the most celebrated lasting 105 days in 1688–89 against the forces of James II. The Walker Monument was destroyed by a bomb in 1973.

**GRAIGUENAMANAGH,
CO. KILKENNY, IN 1926**
The restored Cistercian abbey was
founded by William Marshall in 1207.
The cloister, chapter house and
domestic buildings remain in part,
but are hidden within modern
buildings. The baptistry has a fine
13th century doorway.

SWORDS, CO. DUBLIN
This photograph shows the village and castle on a hot summer's day in
June 1934. The castle was originally built around 1200 as an episcopal
manor for the archbishops of Dublin.

KILLALA, CO. MAYO, ROUND TOWER
Killala, which is 9 kilometres north of
Ballina takes its name from a church
founded here by St Patrick. This
photograph, taken in 1936, shows
the village with its fine 26 metre
high round tower.

INDEX